Renee & Gayle
Gates
Poetic Souls
Ed Hill
Elmer 2014

THE

DESERT

HAT

Survival Poems
By Ed Rosenthal

This book is published by **Moonrise Press**
P.O. Box 4288, Los Angeles – Sunland
CA 91041-4288, www.moonrisepress.com

Prior publication of a version of the poem "My Girl Friend the Canyon" on
the website *DowntownArtWalk.org* and of poems "Brokers of The Downturn"
and a version of "The Voyage" on the website *Tales From Poetic Oceans* is
hereby gratefully acknowledged.

Photos of Salvation Canyon by Ken and Wendy Sims of Sky Valley are used by
permission of authors. Introduction © 2013 by Ruth Nolan is used by
permission of the author.

Photos of Ed Rosenthal and of his "desert hat" by Maja Trochimczyk, taken in
September 2013 in Descanso Gardens, California.
Cover photograph (a dried flower stem of a Mojave Valley Yucca), taken by
Maja Trochimczyk in Big Tujunga Wash, California.

The font Trebuchet MS is used throughout the text, with Arial Black on the title
pages and Calibri in introductions.

Manufactured in the United States of America

The Library of Congress Publication Data:

Rosenthal, Ed, 1947–
 [Poems. English]
 The Desert Hat. Survival Poems / Ed Rosenthal, author
 With an Introduction by Ruth Nolan
        74 pages (60 pp. + xiv pp.) 15.2 cm x 22.9 cm. Written in English.
        Includes 36 poems, 11 photos, a portrait, an introduction and
        acknowledgments.

        ISBN 978-0-9819693-7-4 (paperback)
        I. Rosenthal, Ed, 1947– Poetry. II. Title.

10 9 8 7 6 5 4 3 2 1

THE

DESERT

HAT

Survival Poems
By Ed Rosenthal

Los Angeles   2013

CONTENTS

PREFACE

With great pleasure we present to poetry lovers around the world this debut book of an extraordinary poet, survivor, man, and human being. Ed Rosenthal's first volume of lyrical poetry was inspired by surviving alone in the Mojave Desert for six and a half days. We have no inkling about what he felt and what he saw there, even if we are trying to put ourselves in his shoes.

Moonrise Press is delighted to share this rare find with our readers. Mr. Rosenthal's poetry does not recount his experience in detail; it is not replete with maps, photographs, and a day-by-day account of his adventures. Instead, we gain an insight into what it means to be truly lost and found, to survive the strangest of desert nights and return to the heart of the city... with a newly found wisdom and zest for life.

We would like to thank Ruth Nolan, Professor of English @ College of the Desert, California desert poet, writer, editor, conservationist and scholar, for writing an introduction to this volume. Prof. Nolan is an expert on the literature of California deserts; among other projects, she edited a well-regarded anthology *No Place for a Puritan: the Literature of California's Deserts* (Heyday 2009). We also express our profound gratitude to Suzanne Lummis, a poetry institution of her own, for thoroughly reviewing the entire manuscript and providing many insightful and inspired comments.

The book is illustrated with my photos of Ed Rosenthal's "desert hat," covered with messages to his family, brief poems, the list of his pall-bearers, and fragments of his last will. This hat is a vivid testimony of his state of mind in the desert and an astounding artifact that merits a place in a museum. Surprisingly, none of the poems in the book are direct transcriptions of what he wrote in the desert. Yet another mystery for our readers!

~ Maja Trochimczyk, Ph.D.
President, Moonrise Press

INTRODUCTION

"There is a canyon of pink and
lavender stones.
Walls in tattoos carved by tectonic artists,
say 'Hiker, this is the entry to your quest.'
The air bursts wide."

On an unseasonably hot, late September day in 2010, prolific Los Angeles poet/broker Ed Rosenthal, who had just closed an historic real estate deal in downtown L.A., left the city and took off on a 2-mile hike he'd done numerous times before in the Mojave Desert's Joshua Tree National Park. Little did he know, as he started out for Warren View from Black Rock Campground, on the parks' western edge, that his life was about to dramatically and unalterably change forever.

For the next six days, after taking a wrong turn on his way back to his car, and in temperatures that rose well above the 100-degree mark each day, Rosenthal endured a life and death struggle in a remote, highly inaccessible canyon in one of the Park's most rugged and inhospitable areas. Not only did he run out of water and food within his first few days, but he also lacked most other basic survival supplies, except for his hat and a pen- which he ended up using to write short couplets of encouragement and important messages, including his will for his loved ones.

The story of Rosenthal's disappearance, and survival, after six days alone in the desert's harsh September climate was a story that riveted Southern California's attention - as well as the rest of the nation's - in headlining newspaper and news stories. Like so many others, I anxiously followed the story of his disappearance and the efforts of searchers to find him before it was too late. In addition, as a lifelong, avid back-country Mojave Desert hiker and resident, I was all too aware of the many dangers he faced, especially from exposure and heat. The story of how he was lost, and found, in critical condition but alive, and soon on his way towards making a full recovery, is also a cathartic and transformational one, as rendered here in his own words. "The least I could do, after an experience like this, is write a decent book of poems," he says.

The Desert Hat is a unique desert book, even in a body of desert literature filled with life and death stories of those who have faced the southwestern desert's hostilities. Stories of getting lost, and barely surviving, are staples of the literature of this remotest and most little known of landscapes. For example, William Lewis Manly's famous book *Death Valley in "49,"* which depicts the near-death experience of a party of pioneers who took a wrong turn and barely survived their desert crossing, to the heartbreaking short chapter in Edward Abbey's celebrated memoir *Desert Solitaire,* which provides an intimate portrayal of the author's near-death experience after barely escaping a slot canyon he got trapped in after taking a wrong turn while on a solitary hike.

Like these other desert books, Rosenthal's poetry collection is an entry into another world, into a heightened world of self-reflection, of profound revelations, and spiritual enlightenment; his Mojave is a desert world personified and transformed into a universal place. Of the canyon walls he found himself surrounded by, he writes, *"Those were friends/Stuck in quartz embraces/Veins of orange eyes smiled."* As he wandered and searched for his car, the desert landscape transformed into a place most extraordinary, leaving an indelible impression, as rendered in another poem: *"Ten miles after that turn/The sky was making magic./Turning limbs to ghostly signs/Making a prickly pear look/Like a red shirted hiker."*

These poems are the reader's entry into the "other world" the author himself entered from the moment on a September day when he realized he was lost. In these highly imagistic poems, we are lead along on this most unusual of journeys, which is both a literal and mythopoetic one that can only be rendered by the Mojave's mystical and labyrinthine landscape and through Rosenthal's growing self-awareness and deepening connections with the intimacies of the desert's private nuances, as seen through his eyes and experienced in his imagination during the time he was lost.

From the starting point of this six-day desert odyssey, when Rosenthal took the chance of jumping off of a ravine, through the hours he spent wandering different canyons looking for his way back to his car, to the moments he spent in comradeship with a lone fly, too exhausted to move and facing the possibility that he might not survive, the poems in *The Desert Hat* confirm what desert mystics have always known: that loss, and regeneration of the human spirit, go hand in hand in this loneliest of geographies.

This wonderland of poems will make you cry. It will make you search. It will make you smile, and make you feel a sacred gratitude for your loved ones, and for every desert canyon wall and rock and plant and view of lonely moon that Rosenthal introduces you to, and like him, you will be compelled to contemplate the beauty and tragedy of this harsh place long after you are no longer lost in the desert, but safe at home again.

~ Ruth Nolan
Professor of English @ College of the Desert
California desert poet, writer, editor,
conservationist & scholar

ACKNOWLEDGEMENTS

Thanks to Inland Empire poet Cindy Bousquet Harris and San Gabriel Valley poet Don Kingfisher Campbell for their encouragement. I want to thank Elena Byrne for inspiring me to develop my art.

I cannot thank Maja Trochimczyk of Moonrise Press enough. *The Desert Hat* would never have existed without her. The inspiration for this book is hers.

I'm so honored to have the Mojave Desert poet and advocate Ruth Nolan write the introduction to these poems. Manuscript reviews by iconic LA poet Suzanne Lummis, left me feeling like Homer was on my team.

I must thank my wife Nicole and daughter Hilary for inspiring my survival itself and the poems *The Hat I* and *The Hat II*.

All photos of Salvation Canyon were taken by Ken and Wendy Sims of Sky Valley.

~ Ed Rosenthal

THE

DESERT

HAT

This poem was written in 2009, a year before the event. A fan of Garcia Lorca's poetry, I was fascinated by lunar imagery well before my mis-adventure brought me even closer to the moon.

Brokers of the Downturn

Men in grey slacks sat in silent offices
in a trance they lifted and lowered phones
and watched the white moon shine like ice
above the jade glass tower before them

The blue cobalt stem of his favorite flower
grew from a desk splashed by bronze leaves
meeting vines of dead copper montages
flowering in lead stamens of the brass bulb.

His partners, spread in a maze of partitions
throughout, waited for answers from phones
and watched the moon shine onto the glass
face of the giant jade tower before them

The white face moon pulled him out
upon the board of a purple gang banger
who rode the roof rails down a drain pipe
onto the slope of Bunker Hill to Sixth.

Under the sixth street bridge lights,
cactus suits sporting blossom lapels,
dried sage mustaches and burrs for eyes
plucked high canyon melodies on guitars.

PART ONE

GETTING LOST

POEMS

Alice at Sixty Five - "The Calling"
Burnt Hill - The Debris Trap
Purple Canyon I
Purple Canyon II
Baby Canyon
Moon
The Tree I
The Voyage
The Tree II
Sweet Eyed Boy I
The Tree at Night
Sweet Eyed Boy II

Photo © 2010 by Ken ad Wendy Sims

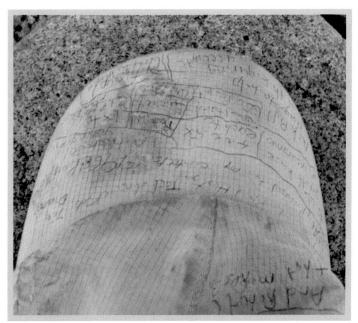

Photo © 2013 by Maja Trochimczyk

Whatever gave me the inclination, to pull away from that cactus, and jump into a new world, on that singular day, usually talks to rocks.

Alice at Sixty Five - "The Calling"

It called me to come down,
come down into the canyon.
You have never been here,
you have never been young.

I slipped down the chute
of dry scrim and sand
and held to the shale sides.
The cactus tangle held me
in a thorny sign of warning.
A branch was my staff,
a branch was my swing
and the disentangled nylon
of yellow sack puffed on my back
when I landed a soft white
place.

Boulders rested halfway
down and waited for storm
waters. I stepped into a world
that was not mine.

Those were friends
stuck in quartz embraces.
Veins of orange eyes smiled
recalling rock memory
born when winter skies
coax stones to smash them
down narrow chutes.

Like heralds of angels
that's where she called me.
She called me down.

There was only one way to escape disaster on the path the hiker mistakenly traveled, an ugly high debris trap.

Burnt Hill

The Debris Trap as Corporate Services

He peered at twiggy ocotillos perched on the rough crown
where ribs of cactus lurked beneath the calcified ground.
The forlorn ridge of leafless twigs projected power down like
corporate logos over elevator lobbies in his home town.

The bony limbs took on the feel of skinny lifeless men
perusing spreadsheets over fat-free cheeses.
Took on the feel of his ex-boss Charles, who allergic to his
wayward leanings, had pushed the hiker on his way.

Filling legs with power, he then ascended the loamy rise,
screaming, pounding his boss's name into the steep hillside,
Cutting his skin to red fish-net stockings covering his thighs,
he climbed up and over the thorn-filled muck of corporate.

Purple Canyon I

Ten miles after that turn,
the sky was magic.
The limbs turned to ghostly signs,
a prickly pear was a red shirted hiker.
Your heart rose when you saw
a huge formation thrust up
from the road bed.
The wash became a wisp of light.

It was not an exit. The road
climbed up a balcony of lost hopes
over a crackling plain of brown grass
clumps. It led you, just then, into
a silent canyon of lavender and rose.
Behind you, your entire life.

Was she
an organ played by the sun
the slates – a purple keyboard?

Was I
her tiny congregation
trudging her turning bottom
lifting my eyes to heaven?

Purple Canyon II

Find the dry falls off the crest of Warren Vista.
Jump down and walk to where you
clutch the trees to keep from falling.
There's no way out but over the debris trap
of muck and thorns due west.
Measure each step so as to not fall
headfirst on Long Valley.

Eleven miles south,
cliff wall barriers rise and fall.
The gathering of pathways,
the unraveling of arroyos
end in one broad sand band
of translucent cholla.
Pink and lavender stones ascend.

Walls in tattoos carved by tectonic artists
say "Hiker, this is the entry to your quest."
The air bursts wide. The path swirls
to white powder drifting
over grey volcanic rock.

You become a child clinging to his mother.

The first night, I still didn't "get" the gravity of my situation.
I had walked twelve miles away from my usual hiking trail,
I was out of water, had lost my sense of direction and it was
a heat wave at the end of the Mojave Desert summer. But
I ended up in this adorable little canyon.

Baby Canyon

Red and blue traces
in the night skies
shot out from the
distant copters.
Running to the cliff
wall, to hold in place
a silver sheet of
emergency blanket
to the pilot's eyes
I flashed my lights
naively - as taught -
three times, three times
hearing my hopes
click click clicking
the switch.

When I dropped
my lights to the sandy floor
I let the dotted
copters and silent jets
go . . .

The Northern Cross floated high
above the flashlight moon
suspended like a cradle toy
over the barren hillside.
Lines of minerals glowed.

The granite-bordered runnel
became the cradle for
my worn bones.

Laying down on the ground
with the black hip of my nylon
pack as a pillow, I let the moon
shine on my bed of silver
emergency cloth, a
metallic hue at the edge
of a bajada, a fifty-mile wide
discarded golf-ball skin.

I fell asleep and dreamt of ice
cream and water jars.

Written immediately after rescue, this child poem revealed my lack of emotional differentiation from the celestial orb.

Moon

When day was night
and dawn was dusk
the moon was the sun
the moon was my compass

When East was West
and North was South
the sun was death
the moon was my mother

The moon told me
I'll stay up high
while you wander
the maze of washes

I'll be up here
white in the blue sky
I'll always be soft
not like your father

Go tramp the East wash
on tiny feet
before he rises
to eclipse me

Hurry through the warren
the marshmallow maze
before he browns them
in canyon anger

Hurry, hurry
but don't fall down
to where neither he
nor I can reach you

The Tree I

The tree spread its branches
over the scrim
green and unbothered
by the white sun climbing its limbs
while the stranger hid
like a neighbor's kid
and slept beneath her branches

The sun pierced her green crown
flinging white heat
from canyon peaks
down through her bowels
at the stranger
entangled

The sky turned bright white
canyon rocks
flashed like desert suns
The sun and the stranger circled

Tree so deep and green
and cool and safe
standing in steep white sand
where men shrink
by your silver trunk
like a seed beneath your skin

The Voyage

The dawn moon told the boy
I'll stay behind you.
Go looking for the canyon
of purple stones along the arroyo.
The one that lifted you
by your boots.

With the moon behind him
he followed the road
over the purple monoliths.
Out the broad mouth the trail spilled
into a place too wide
for the boy.

He turned to ask her
Why am I here?
This is not my Trail
of sheep bones and talc.

Go back again
to the pink spilling
from the feet of your canyon.
Then choose again.

He did, but the trails
turned like rivulets on
a basin of swirled batter,
one as good as another.
He stepped out towards awnings
of white cloud,
to a wide maze of hills
where a hundred trails
meandered.

He stood in a circle of blue
dunes and saw the moon
move on.

The Tree II

White heat flung off canyon peaks,
made a field of relays
from flashing stones.

The chalky canyon was a blur to
the visitor chased by whiteness
into the shadows.

Like a seed pod lying near
the trunk of the isolated
evergreen,

the stranger hid and watched
the sun burn holes
in the sky.

Part of me felt like a little kid lost in a magic place, a little kid befriended by Cholla Cacti, the moon, the evergreen tree and several canyons.

Sweet Eyed Boy I

Go, Little Boy, down to that canyon
where purple granite astounds
where talcum powder sands blow
over grey gumball mounds.
The sheep bone sign to tomorrow
says "boys and girls only."

Where you fell in by accident, Boy,
was once a slide to the past
taken by rocks in a super-size ride
that ended in a mud bath.
At the exit, the white sheep horn cries
"No adults allowed inside."

Go slide the violet face of stones
grown 100,000,000 years ago.
Climb up the busted monster's mouth
of million-year-old crowns.

Stroll *los soldados de cholla verde*
gallery to grab a memory ring
of your friends on the twirling arroyo –
those friends that took you in.

The sheep bone sign to tomorrow
says "boys and girls only."

The Tree at Night

It wasn't a warm light that filled the spaces
of the limbs, curving and pouring around
the silver bark.

Had the moon spread a fountain of blue
over the windy dugout of grey dirt where
the tree lived?

Bordered by faint grass that led to black
darkness, guarded by Joshua trees with
crowns hidden above.

One warned him "Stay away from us,"
showing slivers of his emergency blanket
stuck high up a scaly trunk.

Beneath branches of the tree, blue chills
blew away the memory of daytime's
green shadows.

Sweet Eyed Boy II

I was the world in which I walked, and what I saw
Or heard or felt came not from myself,
And there I found myself more truly and more strange.
  ~ from "Tea at the Palaz of Hoon" by Wallace Stevens

Where you fell in by accident, Boy,
was once a slide to the past,
taken by rocks in a super size ride
that ended in a mud bath.
Your only respite from climbs and falls
was that purple place.

You can't get back to that canyon
of lavender stone
to see talcum powder sands blow
over grey gumball mounds,
where you first felt like
a child again.

But fallen through the bleached
sheep bone signage
of miracle geology park,
you're again,
a wide-eyed boy explorer.

Wear your t-shirted face of six
to slide the violet face of stones
grown 100,000,000 years ago.
Climb up the busted monster's mouth
of million year old crowns.

Cholla cacti surprise you
along the twirling arroyo,
like those boys running games
of housing project tag,
who caught you in passages.

PART TWO

SALVATION CANYON

POEMS

Photo © 2010 by Ken and Wendy Sims

Photo © 2013 by Maja Trochimczyk

Orion on Tuesday

I saw you,
your jeweled belt
your big red eye at dawn,
telling me dawn would come.
Night would end
and begin again
tomorrow.

A warrior, you guard
the seven sisters from
the yellow bull, you
seemed like my mother,
rustling my hair,
putting a blanket
over me.

When I saw you,
taking your place at dawn.

Nearing death, I wondered what my sins were. I felt guilty about a kid named Michael.

Michael

He wasn't like us,
that soft boy
in pressed trousers
who passed us at the fence
walking alone to the concrete platform
for the train to Manhattan.

There he must have read books
with embossed leather covers
and learned things we never would
and run across the sunny plaza
off the sparkling avenue
with the other fine boys with soft manners.
Boys we'd never meet.

Maybe that's why fifty years ago,
during touch football at the park,
when a bunch of us guys surged
against the grey wire fence
of the make believe dugout
behind the imaginary goal line
in the black asphalt park
and I saw him outside the fence,
strolling toward the station
with his leather mahogany case
I pointed him out to a
tough guy from Brooklyn,

"Donny, that kid said you're a moron."

Ode to a Fly

Wonderful insect
may I never see you
stuck to a glue strip
on yellow paper

My sole companion
in Salvation Canyon
you cheerful orange-faced
slender friend

Loyal voyager, we escaped
sand flies, slept on the black rock
and returned to the cliffs
when my Mother in Law
woke up us both
screaming my name
under a black sky

The evolved one
each morning
you hovered to let me
apply lotion then sat
back on my wrist

Dearest Horsefly
Canyon Homemaker
Odd Couple Member
Skinny Legged Friend

The Hat I

I got to the place out of the sun after a three day search
the first day looking for an exit, the second hiding
under a tree, the third morning of survival

A cold moon follows the blistering vision of day
I went downhill for succor, for a friend to lean against
from sun and night wind

In short-sleeve shirt and shorts I had to hide
under a clamshell rock with a split orange face
till the sun slapped me to wake again
I ran in here to the blessed salvation canyon of shadows

Seeing I would outlive that day's sun and maybe
only another, I turned my hat to a mirror
my pen to my blood's red artery

"My dear wife and daughter, I lost the trail of celebration
of deals. I may never see you, read my wish and will."

Out in a desert canyon my love poured onto nylon flaps
inside seams and creases, as the mirror turned into
a bouquet of pomegranates and apricots

for a circle of friends gathered by the barbecue of stewed
tomatoes, candied rice with roasted meats and broiled
fish at my wake of smoking and carousing
with the clink of vodka glasses

per my will, written on my desert hat
to be executed by my beloved
for my only child

Photo © 2013 by Maja Trochimczyk

The Hat II

Slapped by the sun, I slid out of the clamshell rock
to limp into a canyon of shadows,
to hide from sun and night wind in my bare limbed
short sleeves and shorts.

Having delayed my death sentence, by only days,
I saw a short future.

Turning my hat to a notebook,
I poured my love onto nylon.

"My dear wife and daughter, I love you. I lost
my way on my usual trail, I may never see you.
I want a wake and not a funeral.
Don't forget the whitefish and broiled tomatoes."

Visions of my friends turned smoky and crowded
as joints hung from their lips and
tables bursting with pomegranates, and apricots
were circled by drunk guests.

As loved ones came into view, I sent messages,
scribbling like a pattern maker on seams,
creases and crown, the salutations
I'd finish tomorrow.

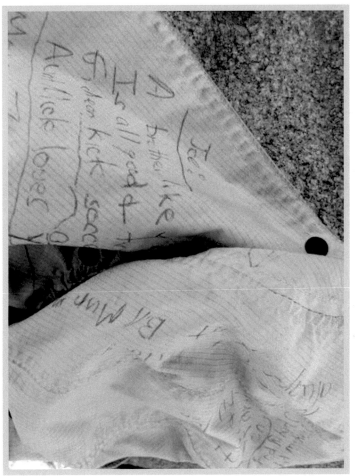

Photo © 2013 by Maja Trochimczyk

I stayed in Salvation Canyon for the last four and a half days in Joshua Tree. It felt like a nurturing place when I was lost there. But when I returned six months later, I had the strangest experience.

My Girl Friend, the Canyon

I was lost till I found your raggedy cliff walls
lined in black shadows. I arrived to see
your walls pour blackness on the ground.

I nestled my shoulders inside the vertices,
lying on my back two feet from harsh light,
squinting at intervals to check the black
shadow of the Acacia.

I'm sorry I set fire to your lacy bush
on the second day. Violet flames lifted, fell,
left a tarry black blemish on you.

We got so close, my things scattered in
your private places. Day and night,
your cliffs kept me from burning heat and cold.

Remember our evenings? My orange pack
beyond the burnt circumference,
beneath the Northern Cross?
I kept your memory in a chrysalis.

Months later, for our reunion,
locals took me under a wire fence,
six miles through bleak limestone drainage,
past a split rock and a coyote squash.

They went to check the entry. They said
a coyote staked it. I was left alone with you.

I thought it would be wonderful to be inside your
precious silence, but gusts of fear filled me.
I froze, unable to turn, look you over.
I blasted my orange whistle.
Panic sent my friends scurrying back.

How I'd kept you in my heart.
But I never really knew you!

You siren that called me down into that dry waterfall,
throwing me like a seed to take root in hell, if I ever saw you,
I would rush to kiss your feet, yelling up to you that it was
worth dying, if only to meet...

Elizabeth B. Moon Canyon

Rise in the road, earthen surprise,
granite winner of awe, inspiration prize
for hikers wandering through this park, found
where searches for exits end after white miles
of boulders line an eternity of broad amber road.
Even from a mile away, your ascending undulations
inspired a completely new view of my prospects
for that ten mile long afternoon.

The road and I became smaller as you became larger,
transformed from a bump on the horizon
to a huge overhang, swallowing the trail itself
where you lifted me up on your curves
to see an unmarked vista of dried creosote bushes,
beneath chalky sky, down haphazard seams
into an endless basin.

When you turned from that massive brown
golf-ball skin of a hillside, you felt like my beloved
teacher, Mrs. Elizabeth Moon, who took me
from the immense blankness of pre-teen boyhood,
to the love of learning, by showing me her heart,
when you showed me your heart

of silence, the chapel where mottled walls
of lavender and rose bore etched tectonic tattoos
across faces riddled by cactus grout, where talcum sands
dusted those ghostly pews of grey gumdrop mounds.
I became your little congregant trudging your bottom.

Your talcum essence stuck to the soles of my boots.
Magically digested by my feet, it traveled upwards
through my entire being, penetrating my heart
in that same secret manner, sixty years after
she left me with a lifelong desire to hold her hand again,
to follow her shadow across wooden classroom floors
become a little part of large things.
I was small again.

You left me branded with a wish to return
to your heart. After a week in a furnace
bookended by unsafe vertices, cruel precipices,
a last minute door of death rescue, the rush
to the emergency room and a miraculous
family reunion,

I was left only crying for you,
you

Rescue Angels

Friday, September 24th

Flying the sky, giant bobbin bees with maroon eyes
buzzed black antennas to stir up the moon.
Secretive Joshua Trees stood like Rodin marble,
mute sentries of the arroyo, pointing nowhere.

The orange-suited searchers didn't think
of this distant canyon, beyond trackless wasteland.
An ocean away, I flashed my amber lights and
whistled my tangerine whistle at the moon.

Thursday, September 30th

Grizzled trackers came out for the search
to paw and grumble at red and black pebbles,
to listen with inner ears for coyote scratches
or hunches of the withered moon.

The coyote's shadow landed on the sheriff's vest
filling his heart with ancient, magic thoughts.
He felt the pull of haphazard fate, pointing south
to my tracks in the cracked terrain of desert
where I was sand in the hourglass of summer.

PART THREE

BACK IN TOWN

POEMS

Photo © 2010 by Ken & Wendy Sims

Photo © 2013 by Maja Trochimczyk

Her Husband

It's like spying on myself,
hearing my wife on the phone.
It doesn't sound
as if she's talking about me
but this guy, "her husband."

Lost in the desert, he was
that sound. What people knew
about me was what they knew
about him, the evidence:
"My husband does not go
off to explore new trails."

The radio signaled over
the Inland Empire morning news
that the hiker's wife said:
"My husband never calls
on hikes, so this was normal.
It had been normal, but before,
my husband always returned."

After the helicopter pilot
lifted me up over the morning
moon, I rested gratefully.
Staring at Intensive Care T.V.
I saw the husband's wife,
smiling above the podium.

My love for nature blossomed from my experience. What about my feelings for those creatures for whom the park is named, those Joshua Trees?

Big Weird and Strange

The second night out made it all clear,
I wanted nothing to do with those
brooding Joshua Trees.

When evening came to tree canyon, my
silver foil emergency blanket tattered
and blew off my legs like a sail.

Taking an aluminum flight past the tree,
it stuck on a forbidding line of clustered
scimitar limbs in a grove.

Avoiding the gnarled giants in the dark,
I kept the tree between myself
and those mysterious beings.

Wrapping my arms and legs in
toilet paper, I slept, and twisted like
a shocked mummy.

Back In Town

Now that I'm not sleeping on the ground
or writing on my hat, unsure if I might die
or talking to a fly, the only friend I found

the helicopter to the hospital complex
shunned his orange face and the nurses
urged him to leave on his threads of legs

my words hover outside ears of deaf
landlords downtown who don't hear
clumps of grass crying in hoarse sand
but think a yellow bulb of a prickly pear
has a tax avoidance plan.

The rib cage and a big sheep face frowned
across the talcum canyon chewed by desert
creatures to a monument of bones
framed by flourishes of pebbles.

I passed it twice on my wandering rounds.

Already in a daze, I wondered what the Sheriff was talking about.

Bagel Shock

On my first trip back to the Mojave
the highway signs looked like
looping Cholla Cactus, the broad asphalt
might lead to a near-death experience.

Breathing heavily, I reach
the meeting hall, thrilled to step into
the room of orange shirts,
my arms filled with plastic bags
of bagels and lox schmear.

Sharing the lox, assorted bagels
onion, mixed and plain, I start to thank
the Desert Search and Rescue
when he pops in, uninvited,
turning heads like Joshua Trees.

A uniformed sheriff, a blond apparition
above the room of orange shoulders
he points at me, words blurting out,
his young moon face flushed with red pride.

"Hey, those guys that saved you
were from my division and they went
against orders."

He leaves without telling me how or why
searchers shifted south
in the white landscape of the moon
sniffing along the winding seams
snatching me up like a plant
of the great Mojave.

Four months after the experience, I thought a lot about spectral presences.

Shadows I

Shadows stretch to listen in the night
for changes in relationships
they'd been anticipating
since turning to ethereal beings
and leaving their mass behind
long ago

Laying on top of a couple
they once hung out with
before opting for the narrow profile
two shadows mixed into one black cover
over the white metal table
lit by red heat lamps
where their old friends sat
covering the right arm
of one buddy
as he lifted the coffee cup
to his lips

Each wondered in silence
if they'd hear any hint
of a change in relatedness
role reversal or new goals
which they, mature shadow sleuths
might record
and upon recording
might accrete to them
so they might gain mass again
now that they were so bored
with slenderness

Purple Canyon III

Looking back at burnt Mojave

the sky turned limbs to ghostly signs.
A prickly pear was a red shirted hiker.

The path circled a plain
of brown clumps, then met
a silent canyon of purple stones.

A week later
after lying like a lifeless log
in a furnace, the pilot's arms
scooped me off the pebbled surface,
I was lifted from death.

The sorrow of my wife and daughter
brought no tears to my eyes.

I cried
for slates of hard rock
encrusted with lavender striations
that broke the curve of earth
to ride the sky in a winding line.

Shadows II

He became a shadow that listened
for clues, for new wisdom, before
he left his mass behind

Like a black shade,
sitting at a white table,
covering a buddy's arm
and part of a coffee cup

Wondering in silence if he'd hear
hints of changes in his friend
which he might credit to his own
tale of near death

PART FOUR

REFLECTIONS

POEMS

Helicopter Landing Site in Salvation Canyon
Photo © 2010 by Ken and Wendy Sims

45

Photo © 2013 by Maja Trochimczyk

O'Connor

It was just another day, the last time I saw
O'Connor. The steel trestle arching
over roiled green waters to the reedy peninsula
of stilt houses where he lived. Him taking off
for the walkways on the marsh. Grey seagulls
squawking on wobbly handrails.
A smile lifted dimples to his eyes, "Hey,
I'm not coming back to school. "

I should have hugged him, pulling his jacket
to cover his open neck from salt winds,
kissed him like boys don't, for the shocked
English teacher's face, the curses
scribbled white on the blackboard,
the Principal's shrieks in the hallway.

When snows turn the marshes white the
stalks of salt reeds crack with shanty rumors.
Barely heard sneakers in wet bay snow. Melted
footprints on the slushy boardwalk.
Hushed whispers say, "When summer burns
the green reeds gold, he'll be gone."

Neocon Blue

Green how I want you green. green wind. Green branches.
The ship on the sea And the horse on the mountain.
                              ~ Garcia Lorca, Havard

Blue I don't want you
Blue curses. Blue truths
Storms on the blue lake
cast waves to the sky.
The lifeguard slides down
the snowy mountains
to the delta.
Hidden in the white
snow rifts, depressed
philosophers slide with
heads upside down.

Blue how I hate you blue
Floating along the Potomac
boatloads of metallic
etchings portraying children
swept from school yards,
barriers across
hospitals, blue nuns
blown up chimneys,
blue pin stripes
flown in on brooms.

I was like you Mr. Blue
in freshman summer,
I cuddled with Iron Ayn's
novels, but now
bloated Mooches
swim up pool ladders
from sewers
to high Washington
verandas.

A blue flag swirling in
red flames, exploding
stars and cocaine bars.

Above the prison catwalk,
blue blouses stained
in scarlet varnish.
Neon eye lids
stuffed in blue hoods
scan sulfurous
neighborhood streets.

The Statue of Liberty
goes for a swim.
In the ballroom,
the blind accountant
dispenses eviction notices.

The Visitor

My evaporated spine left me a crab crawling over sand to the granite barrier where a marble figure with royal bearing, thrust up in a short skirt and sandals.

Asking him what to do, I watched the canyon walls shrink and the ledge turn to a shrine. Drops fell in the pink morning.

He felt like the presence who appeared above the bureau, radiating love through that cheap hotel room where the factory owners stuck me in that summer of melted asphalt,

who came a decade later in a silver uniform on a silver bike with a silver cross on the wheel cover, to stop all six lanes of traffic on the freeway and take my dead car across to safety. He left without a word,

But I'm a Jew, so I crawled like a wounded servant back to the other side. I dug Hebrew words from memory, to pray to Yahva to finish what the visitor had started.

I lay back with my arms outstretched and felt the waters line my face. I watched for the apparition, my possessions gathered around me in a halo. I fell asleep. Raindrops fell. The sky flashed from misty white to dark gray.

Back downtown, a panhandler popped out of the sidewalk, shocking me with intimacy: "Hey, you that broker that was lost last year?"

I nodded.

"I prayed for you."

"Thank you," I responded.

"Never mind that, you remember yet who saved you in the canyon?"

"No, I don't," I replied.

"No? Well, you better think about it."

Is This Why It Happened, after Decades of Hiking the Same Trail to Warren View?

Each year, a man returns to the same hotel room
but never knows why.

He sits enchanted on a hillside, pondering peaks
beyond the desert floor, when an angel
fills his guts with bliss.

Unclear as a drunk of the genesis of desire,
he lets hill tops of bending grass,
echo-locate him like a beacon.

To the same viewpoint of green foothills,
the plain of dried grasses, mountain twins
at the rim of the horizon.

After decades of reunions, the angel wants
him to get off his viewpoint and
throws his soul a curve

leading him down a rocky waterfall,
to jump or tumble where broken rocks
glow like filaments.

Desert Fruits I

He never saw
petals of giant Saguaro, stick white tongues from fluffy
stamens, or Cholla's cups of orange honey, no blooms of the
pincushion cacti, circling spines like a tiara. The undulating
bajada was not a sea of flashing brittlebush caps.

He never saw
pistachio petals dance on cactus limbs. Those gentlemen
Cholla had no gloves and no ochre corsage finery. No fiery
roses on the staghorn's limbs. Dirty hedge hogs hid in shadows.

The Yucca he found
without purple and eggshell nuts, had no flowery wands.
Lying low and building up a seasonal spike. Cutting its trunk
only tired his arms and all pulled out fronds burnt in the walk
downhill.

But after he, a dried

Seed, was propagated by helicopter winds, he became a
wounded flower.

Return

Now that I'm not sleeping on the ground
or writing on my hat, or talking to a fly,
I'm back.

The fly never boarded the copter to the
hospital grounds.

At best, he'd be left hovering like my tale
hangs outside ears of friends,

the one about that bleached horn and
sheep bones on the ground,

flashing blessings for we who have not
crossed over,

I passed them twice on wandering rounds.

Desert Fruits II

He never saw
the billowing petals of the giant Saguaro blossoms, sticking
luscious white tongues from fluffy yellow stamens, or Cholla's
glowing cups of orange blossom honey, the lily blooms
of the pincushion cacti, circling the spines like a bride's tiara.
The undulating bajada was not a folding sea of golden
brittlebush caps, flashing.

He never saw
pistachio petals lying like tiny water lilies in zigzags of green
Cholla. The gentlemen Cholla hid instead of bending white
gloved spines, showing off ochre corsages to beetles. No stag
horn cactus lifted an orange rose in the dry furnace, while
browned hedge hogs were hiding in flowerless creosote, in
Joshua Tree.

The Yucca he found
had no creamy blossoms shooting out along the green stem.
It was not announcing its renewed energy by waving purple
and white tuxedo nuts over the desert in flowery wands.
Not when he found it, lying low and gathering cellular
building blocks for a later spike.

He couldn't have
known without seeing inside cell walls, that cutting its
waterless trunk only tired his raised arms and the dry fronds
he succored would burn in the steep walk downhill.

After heat
and dehydration dried him to the seed of a tiny boy and he was
propagated by helicopter winds to the hospital, he himself
became soft petals of a wounded flower, cupped in black
stems of the admitting Nurse arms. Downturned stamens
of pink and cobalt fruits fertilized him, held by electric
filament around his spine inside

The hospital oasis.

Coyote

You stood blocking the trail marker
where I dropped from sight that day.
Ineligible shaman signal, I thought
you random as the park pump by
the hidden sky of water tower.

Lifted out by copter wings, pumped
by hospital fluids, when I got home,
I found you illustrated in my room.
Inside a copper band of a silver ring
I had left unworn ten years.

It won't come off my finger.

THE END

ABOUT THE AUTHOR

Photo © 2013 by Maja Trochimczyk

Ed Rosenthal, Survivor

Ed Rosenthal, "Poet/Broker of Downtown Los Angeles," was known for using his verses to keep his escrows going. Taking the opposite tact of iconic modernist poets Wallace Stevens and T.S. Eliot, who kept their day jobs at a seeming distance from their poetry, "Poet/Broker" employed poetry as a tool in commercial real estate. Rosenthal's "Poetic Request for 30 day Extension of Contingencies" was cited in the *Los Angeles Times* for enabling a redevelopment project. His *Wall Street Journal* piece admonished clients in couplets. To place poetic legitimacy on his state-issued real estate licenses, Rosenthal had some signed by world renowned writers, including Seamus Heaney and Evan Boland.

Prior to his near-death experience, he was already bored with the persona of the "Poet/Broker." A fan of Federico Garcia Lorca, Rosenthal began to work with poems carrying lunar motifs in urban landscapes. Survival of a harrowing near-death experience in the Mojave Desert in 2010 has deepened this imagistic writer's divorce from practicality in the direction of spiritual exploration.